# World's Best Funny Songs

BY ESTHER L. NELSON

ILLUSTRATIONS BY JOYCE BEHR

 Sterling Publishing Co., Inc.   New York

# Acknowledgments

Thank you to Risa Sokolsky, Sheila Gladstone and Hannah Reich. And another thanks to my doubly unique editor and friend Sheila Anne Barry for this, our tenth collaboration.

**Library of Congress Cataloging-in-Publication Data**

The World's best funny songs.

  Melodies with chord symbols.
  Includes indexes.
  Summary: Presents the lyrics, melody lines, and guitar chords to over sixty humorous songs.
  1. Children's songs.  2. Humorous songs—Juvenile.  [1. Humorous songs.  2. Songs.]
I. Nelson, Esther L.  II. Behr, Joyce, ill.
M1997.W895   1988       87-753871
ISBN 0-8069-6770-6
ISBN 0-8069-6771-4 (lib. bdg.)

The material in this collection has been excerpted from the following books copyrighted by Esther L. Nelson and published by Sterling Publishing Co., Inc.: The Fun-to-Sing Songbook © 1986, The Great Rounds Songbook © 1985, The Funny Songbook © 1984, The Silly Songbook © 1981.

Music copying by Glen Vecchione

Additional material and arrangements © 1988
ISBN 0-8069-6893-1 (pbk.)

3    5    7    9    10    8    6    4

Published in 1988 by Sterling Publishing Co., Inc.
387 Park Avenue South, New York, N.Y. 10016
Distributed in Canada by Sterling Publishing
% Canadian Manda Group, P.O. Box 920, Station U
Toronto, Ontario, Canada M8Z 5P9
Distributed in Great Britain and Europe by Cassell PLC
Artillery House, Artillery Row, London SW1P 1RT, England
Distributed in Australia by Capricorn Ltd.
P.O. Box 665, Lane Cove, NSW 2066
*Manufactured in the United States of America*
*All rights reserved*

Here's to you, Ruth Orlofsky—for your wealth of spirit and your unique melody.

# CONTENTS

# 1. THE SILLIEST SONGS IN THE WORLD

# Around the Corner

Around the corner
And under a tree,
A sergeant major
Once said to me,
"Who would marry you,
I would like to know,
For every time
I look at your face
It makes me want to go
Around the corner
          *(and on and on and on).*

A-round the cor - ner, —— and un-der a tree, A ser-geant ma-jor,—once said to me: "Who would mar-ry you? I would like to know, For ev'ry time I look at your face it makes me want to go A-round the cor - ner,"—— and un-der a tree *(and so on).*

# John Jacob Jingleheimer Schmidt

John Jacob Jingleheimer Schmidt—
His name is my name, too.
Whenever we go out,
The people always shout:
"There goes John Jacob
    Jingleheimer Schmidt"
Dah, dah, dah, dah, dah,
    dah, dah,"

    *(and on and on and on).*

John Ja-cob Jing-le-heim-er Schmidt —

His name is my name, too. When-

ev-er we go out, the peo-ple al-ways shout:"There goes

John Ja - cob Jing - le - heim - er

Schmidt," dah dah dah dah dah dah dah,

# Up in the Air, Junior Bird Man

Up in the air, Junior Bird Man,
Up in the air, Bird Man true!
Up in the air, Junior Bird Man,
Keep your eyes up in the blue!
(Up in the blue!)

And when you hear that grand announcement,
Then we will all have wings of tin,
And you can bet your Junior Bird Men
will send their boxtops in!

It takes just four---------
Boxtops

*(Do this part
with gestures—*
*see page 11)*

And six---------
Bottle bottoms!

    (*spoken*)  Whoooooooooosssssssshhhhhhh!

Bird Man, keep your eyes up in the blue! (up in the blue!) And when you hear that grand an-nounce-ment, then we will all have wings of tin, and you can bet your Jun-ior Bird Men — will send their box-tops in! It takes just four — box-tops and six — bot-tle bot-toms!

# Aiken Drum

There was a man lived in the moon,
Lived in the moon, lived in the moon.
There was a man lived in the moon,
And his name was Aiken Drum.


**Chorus**
And he played upon a ladle,
            a ladle, a ladle,
And he played upon a ladle,
And his name was Aiken Drum.

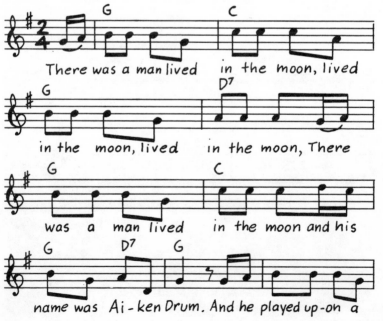

There was a man lived in the moon, lived in the moon, lived in the moon, There was a man lived in the moon and his name was Ai-ken Drum. And he played up-on a

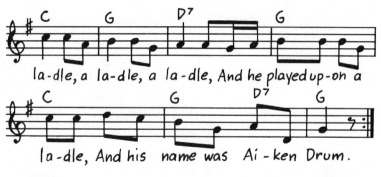

la-dle, a la-dle, a la-dle, And he played up-on a

la-dle, And his name was Ai-ken Drum.

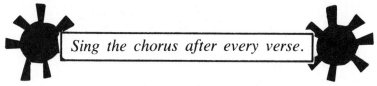

*Sing the chorus after every verse.*

And his hat was made of pudding,
            of pudding, of pudding,
And his hat was made of pudding,
And his name was Aiken Drum.


And his coat was made of turkey,
            of turkey, of turkey,
And his coat was made of turkey,
And his name was Aiken Drum.


And his belt was made of licorice,
            of licorice, of licorice,
And his belt was made of licorice,
And his name was Aiken Drum.


And his pants were made of fish sticks,
            of fish sticks, of fish sticks,
And his pants were made of fish sticks
And his name was Aiken Drum.

And his buttons were made of walnuts,
   of walnuts, of walnuts,
And his buttons were made of walnuts,
And his name was Aiken Drum.

And his hair was made of spaghetti,
   of spaghetti, of spaghetti,
And his hair was made of spaghetti,
And his name was Aiken Drum.

And his eyes were made of jelly beans,
   of jelly beans, of jelly beans,
And his eyes were made of jelly beans,
And his name was Aiken Drum.

And his mouth was made of marshmallow,
   of marshmallow, of marshmallow,
And his mouth was made of marshmallow,
And his name was Aiken Drum.

And his nose was made of nose drops,
   of nose drops, of nose drops,
And his nose was made of nose drops,
And his name was Aiken Drum.

# Old MacTavish Is Dead

Old MacTavish is dead, and his brother
don't know it.
His brother is dead and MacTavish don't
know it.
They're both of them dead, and they're in
the same bed—
So neither one knows that the other is
dead!

# One Bottle Pop

One bottle pop,
Two bottle pop,
Three bottle pop,
Four bottle pop,
Five bottle pop,
Six bottle pop,
Seven bottle bottle pop,

Fish and chips and vinegar,
Vinegar, vinegar.
Fish and chips and vinegar.
Pepper pepper pepper salt.

One bot-tle pop, Two bot-tle pop, Three bot-tle pop,

Four bot-tle pop, Five bot-tle pop, Six bot-tle pop,

Sev-en bot-tle bot-tle pop.   Fish and chips and

vin - e - gar, vin - e - gar, vin - e - gar,

Fish and chips and vin - e - gar, pep-per pep-per pep-per

salt. Don't throw your trash in my back yard,

my back yard, my back yard, Don't throw your trash in

my back yard, my back yard's full!

Don't throw your trash in my back yard,
My back yard, my back yard
Don't throw your trash in my back yard
My back yard's full!

# I With I Were

I with I were a fith-y in the thea
      (in the thea),
I with I were a fith-y in the thea
      (in the thea),
I would thwimmy 'round tho cute-y,
      (without a bathing thuit-y),
I with I were a fith-y in the thea.

I with I were a wittle thugar bun (thugar bun),
I with I were a wittle thugar bun (thugar bun),
I would thlip-y and I'd thlide-y
　　　down everyone's inthide-y,
I with I were a wittle thugar bun.


I with I were a wittle cake of thoap
　　　(cake of thoap),
I with I were a wittle cake of thoap
　　　(cake of thoap),
I would thlip-y and I'd thlide-y
　　　on everybody's hide-y,
I with I were a wittle cake of thoap.


I with I were a wittle thlippery thlime
　　　(thlippery thlime),
I with I were a wittle thlippery thlime
　　　(thlippery thlime),
I would ooze-y, ooze-y, ooze-y
　　　in everybody's shoes-ies,
I with I were a wittle
　　　thlippery thlime.

I with I were a wittle mothquito
        (mothquito),
I with I were a wittle mothquito
        (mothquito),
I would buzz-y and I'd bite-y
        through everybody's nightie,
I with I were a wittle mothquito.

I with I were a wittle thafety pin
        (thafety pin),
I with I were a wittle thafety pin
        (thafety pin),
I'd get cruthty and I'd rutht-y
        until everything went butht-y,
I with I were a wittle thafety pin.

I with I weren't thuch a thilly thimp
        (thilly thimp),
I with I weren't thuch a thilly thimp
        (thilly thimp),
I'd thing a thuper thong that made thenth
        and wathn't w'ong,
I with I weren't thuch a thilly thimp.

# 2. JIGSAW SONGS

The songs in this section are jigsaw songs. Each time you sing them, you leave out another word until almost nothing is left. Then you put the words back and sing the song again. It's like breaking apart and rebuilding a jigsaw puzzle.

# John Brown's Baby

## *(To the tune of "Battle Hymn of the Republic")*

John Brown's baby
Had a cold upon his chest,
John Brown's baby
Had a cold upon his chest,
John Brown's baby
Had a cold upon his chest,
And they rubbed it in
With camphorated oil.

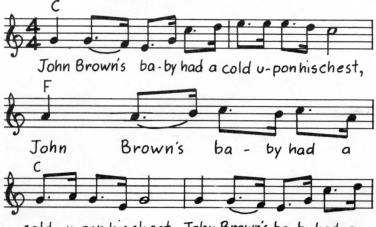

John Brown's ba-by had a cold u-pon his chest, John Brown's ba-by had a cold u-pon his chest, John Brown's ba-by had a

cold   u-pon  his  chest,      and  they

G⁷                                C

rubbed  it  in  with  cam-phor - a - ted   oil.

First sing the song without motions. The second time, leave out the word "baby" in every line and make believe you're rocking a baby in your arms instead. The third time, in addition to "baby," leave out the word "cold." Sneeze, cough or shake your head instead. The fourth time, besides "baby" and "cold," tap your chest with a loud thud instead of saying "chest." The fifth time, leave out "rubbed it in" and rub your chest in a circle instead. Finally, leave out camphorated oil: instead hold your nose (it smells bad).

John Brown's _____ had a _____ upon his_____,
              (rock)        (cough)             (tap)

John Brown's _____ had a _____ upon his_____,
              (rock)        (cough)             (tap)

John Brown's _____ had a _____ upon his_____,
              (rock)        (cough)             (tap)

And they _____ with _____.
           (rub it in)          (hold nose)

# Little Peter Rabbit

### *(To the tune of "Battle Hymn of the Republic")*

Little Peter Rabbit had a fly upon his ear,
Little Peter Rabbit had a fly upon his ear,
Little Peter Rabbit had a fly upon his ear,
And he flicked it till it flew away.


_____ Peter _____ had a _____ upon his _____,
(show size)      (chew carrot)      (swat)      (ear)

_____ Peter _____ had a _____ upon his _____,
(show size)      (chew carrot)      (swat)      (ear)

_____ Peter _____ had a _____ upon his _____,
(show size)      (chew carrot)      (swat)      (ear)

And he flicked it till it flew away.

# Oh, Chester!

Oh, Chester, have you heard about Harry—
Just got back from the army,
I hear he knows how to wear his clothes—
Hip hip hooray for the army!

Oh, _____ er, have _____ _____ about _____ —
  (slap chest)          (point)  (cup ear)        (pull hair)

Just got _____ from the _____ ,
     (slap back)       (slap arm, then chest—*arm-me*)

I _____ he _____ how to _____ —
(cup ear)    (tap nose)     (both hands gesture down,
                           up, and down sides)

_____ _____ hooray for the _____ !
(slap hip) (slap other hip)        (slap arm, then chest—*arm-me*)

# Bingo Was His Name

There was a farmer had a dog,
And Bingo was his name, sir.
B-I-N-G-O,
B-I-N-G-O,
B-I-N-G-O,
And Bingo was his name, sir.

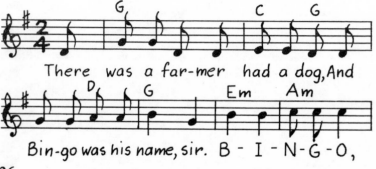

B - I - N - G-O, B - I - N-G-O And Bin-go was his name, sir.

There was a farmer had a dog,
And Bingo was his name, sir.
(*Clap*) I-N-G-O,
(*Clap*) I-N-G-O,
(*Clap*) I-N-G-O
And Bingo was his name, sir.

There was a farmer had a dog,
And Bingo was his name, sir.
(*Clap, clap*) N-G-O,
(*Clap, clap*) N-G-O,
(*Clap, clap*) N-G-O
And Bingo was his name, sir.

There was a farmer had a dog,
And Bingo was his name, sir.
(*Clap, clap, clap*) G-O,
(*Clap, clap, clap*) G-O,
(*Clap, clap, clap*) G-O
And Bingo was his name, sir.

There was a farmer had a dog,
And Bingo was his name, sir.
(*Clap, clap, clap, clap*) O,
(*Clap, clap, clap, clap*) O,

(*Clap, clap, clap, clap*) O
And Bingo was his name, sir.

There was a farmer had a dog,
And Bingo was his name, sir.
(*Clap, clap, clap, clap, clap*)
(*Clap, clap, clap, clap, clap*)
(*Clap, clap, clap, clap, clap*)
And Bingo was his name, sir.

The farmer's dog's at our back door,
Beggin' for a bone, sir.
B-I-N-G-O,
B-I-N-G-O,
B-I-N-G-O
And Bingo was his name, sir.

# 3. OH—GROSS!

# Greasy, Grimy Gopher Guts

*(To the tune of "The Old Grey Mare")*

Great green globs of greasy grimy gopher guts,
Mutilated monkey's meat,
Little birdie's dirty feet,
Great green globs of greasy grimy gopher guts,
And I forgot my spoon!

Great green gobs of greas-y grim-y go-pher guts

mu-ti-la-ted mon-key meat, lit-tle bird-ie's dir-ty feet

Great green gobs of greas-y grim-y go-pher guts and

I for-got my spoon!

# Mud, Mud, Glorious Mud

Mud, mud, glorious mud,
Nothing quite like it for
  cooling your blood.
Follow me, follow,
Down to the hollow,
Where we will wallow
In glorious mud.

Mud, mud, glo - ri - ous mud,

No-thing quite like it for cool-ing your blood,

Fol-low me, fol-low, Down to the hol-low,

Where we will wal-low in glo-ri-ous mud.

# My Father Hunted a Kangaroo

My father hunted a kangaroo,
Just for a grizzly end to chew.
Wasn't that a terrible thing to do?
To hunt just to chew the grizzly end
    of a slew kangaroo.

# I'm Being Eaten
# By a Boa Constrictor

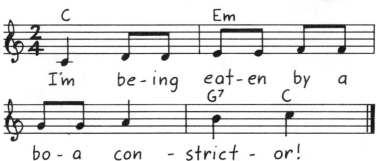

I'm being eaten by a boa constrictor—
(*spoken*) Oh no, he's got my toe!
Oh gee, he's got my knee!
Oh my, he's got my thigh!
Oh yip, he's got my hip!
Make haste, he's got my waist!
Be calm, he's got my arm!

That's grand, he's got my hand!
That bum, he's got my thumb!
Oh yes, he's got my chest!
Oh heck, he's got my neck!
Hey, Ted, he's got my head!
    Hemahonahoomangrahg . . . .

# The Old Family Toothbrush

The old family toothbrush,
That dirty old toothbrush,
That slimy old toothbrush
That hangs on the wall.

Oh, first it was Father's,
And then it was Mother's,
And next it was Sister's
And now it is mine.

Oh, Father he used it,
And Mother abused it,
And Sister refused it,
And now it is mine.

The old family toothbrush,
That dirty old toothbrush,
That slimy old toothbrush
That hangs on the wall.

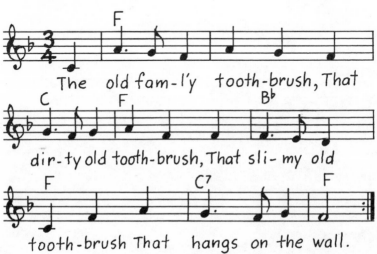

The old fam-l'y tooth-brush, That
dir-ty old tooth-brush, That sli-my old
tooth-brush That hangs on the wall.

# Dirty Bill

I know a man named Dirty Bill,
Lives in a house on Garbage Hill,
Never took a bath and never will.
Oigh, foigh, Dirty Bill!

I know a man named Dir-ty
Bill, Lives in a house on
Gar-bage Hill, Ne-ver took a
bath and ne-ver will. *(spoken)*
Oigh, foigh, Dir-ty Bill!

# Dear Old Daddy's Whiskers

We have a dear old Daddy
Whose hair is silver gray.
He has a set of whiskers—
They're always in the way.

We have a dear old Dad-dy, whose

hair is sil-ver gray. He has a set of

whis-kers, They're al-ways in the way, Oh they're

al-ways in the way, The cow eats them for

hay, Mo-ther eats them in her sleep, She

thinks she's eat-ing shred-ded wheat, They're

al - ways     in     the     way.

**Chorus**

Oh, they're always in the way.
The cow eats them for hay.
Mother eats them in her sleep,
She thinks she's eating shredded wheat,
They're always in the way.

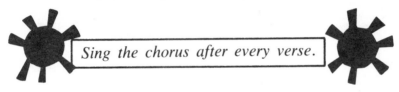

*Sing the chorus after every verse.*

We have a dear old Mommy,
She likes his whiskers, too.
She uses them for cleaning
And stirring up a stew.


We have a dear old brother,
Who has a Ford machine.
He uses Daddy's whiskers
To strain the gasoline.


We have a dear old sister.
It really is a laugh.
She sprinkles Daddy's whiskers
As bath salts in her bath.

We have another sister,
Her name is Ida Mae.
She climbs up Daddy's whiskers
And braids them every day.

Around the supper table,
We make a merry group,
Until dear Daddy's whiskers
Get tangled in the soup.

Daddy was in battle,
He wasn't killed, you see:
His whiskers looked like bushes,
And fooled the enemy.

When Daddy goes in swimming,
No bathing suit for him.
He ties his whiskers 'round his waist,
And happily jumps in.

The hottest days of summer
Are getting pretty good,
'Cause Daddy waves his whiskers
And cools the neighborhood.

# Dunderbeck's Machine

There was a man from Pleasantville,
His name was Dunderbeck.
He sold a lot of sausages
And sauerkraut, by heck.
He made the greatest sausages
That you have ever seen
Until one day he invented
A sausage meat machine.

### Chorus

Oh, Dunderbeck, oh, Dunderbeck,
How could you be so mean?
To ever have invented
Such a terrible machine?
Now alley cats and long-tailed rats
Will never more be seen.
They'll all be ground to sausage meat
In Dunderbeck's machine!

*Sing the chorus after every verse.*

One day a little fat boy came
A-walking in the store.
He bought a pound of sausages
And laid them on the floor.
Then he began to whistle,
He whistled up a tune.
The sausages they jumped and barked
And danced around the room.

One day the thing got busted.
The darn thing wouldn't work,
And Dunderbeck he crawled inside
To see what made it jerk.
His wife came walking in just then
Cause she walked in her sleep,
She gave the crank a heck of a yank,
And Dunderbeck was meat!

So, if you have a cat or dog,
You better keep it locked.
'Cause if you don't. I'm warning you,
You're in for some big shock.
If ever you eat some sausage meat
From Dunderbeck right now,
You'll hear the little sausages
Meow and bow-wow-wow!

# The Little Skunk Hole

Oh, I stuck my head
In the little skunk hole,
And the little skunk said,
"Well, bless my soul!
Take it out! Take it out! Take it out!
TAKE IT OUT!
REMOVE IT!"

Oh, I stuck my head in the lit-tle skunk

hole, And the lit-tle skunk said "Well bless my

soul, Take it out! Take it out! Take it

out! TAKE IT OUT, RE-MOVE IT!"

Well, I didn't take it out,
And the little skunk said,
"If you don't take it out,
You'll wish you were dead.
Take it out! Take it out!
   Take it out!

(*holding nose*) Pee-yoo!
   I removed it

(*spoken*) TOOOO LATE!!!!!!!!!!

# The Quartermaster Corps

Oh, it's beans, beans, beans,
That turn us into fiends
In the corps, in the corps.
Oh, it's beans, beans, beans,
That turn us into fiends,
In the Quartermaster Corps.

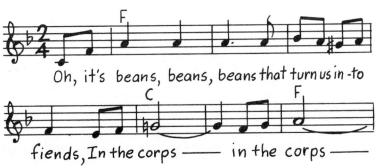

Oh, it's beans, beans, beans that turn us in-to
fiends, In the corps —— in the corps ——

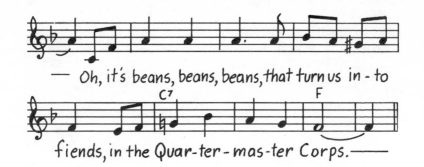

— Oh, it's beans, beans, beans, that turn us in-to

fiends, in the Quar-ter-mas-ter Corps. —

### Chorus

Mine eyes are dim;
I cannot see.
I have not brought my specs with me.

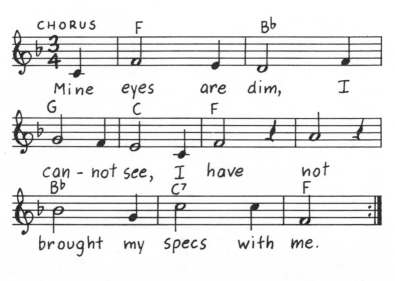

CHORUS

Mine eyes are dim, I can-not see, I have not brought my specs with me.

*Sing the chorus after every verse.*

Oh, it's soup, soup, soup,
That knocks you for a loop
In the corps, in the corps,
Oh, it's soup, soup, soup
That knocks you for a loop
In the Quartermaster Corps.

Oh, it's cheese, cheese, cheese,
That brings you to your knees
In the corps, in the corps. (*Repeat*)

Oh, it's meat, meat, meat,
That isn't fit to eat
In the corps, in the corps. (*Repeat*)

Oh, it's peas, peas, peas,
That make you want to sneeze
In the corps, in the corps. (*Repeat*)

Oh, it's stew, stew, stew,
That turns you black and blue
In the corps, in the corps. (*Repeat*)

Oh, it's bread, bread, bread,
Sits in your gut like lead
In the corps, in the corps. (*Repeat*)

Oh, it's cake, cake, cake,
That makes your stomach ache
In the corps, in the corps. (*Repeat*)

Oh, it's pears, pears, pears,
That give you curly hairs
In the corps, in the corps. (*Repeat*)

Oh, it's pie, pie, pie,
That hits you in the eye
In the corps, in the corps. (*Repeat*)

# 4. RIDICULOUS ROUNDS

# Benjy Met a Bear

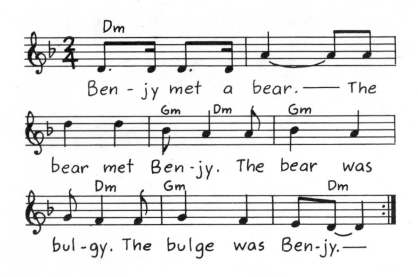

Ben - jy met a bear.—— The
bear met Ben-jy. The bear was
bul-gy. The bulge was Ben-jy.——

Benjy met a bear.
The bear met Benjy.
The bear was bulgy.
The bulge was Benjy.

# The Pizza Round

I've got a sausage pizza in my 12-string case
And an E-string in my shoe.
There's a blind, purple people-eater in my bed.
Now what am I to do?

# Lazy Fred

Here lie the bones of lazy Fred,
Who wasted precious time in bed.
Some plaster fell upon his head,
And, Lord be praised, our Freddie's dead.

# Thirty Purple Birds

*Plain version:*
Thirty purple birds,
Sitting on the curb,
A-chirping and a-burping
And a-chewing dirty worms.

Thir-ty pur-ple birds, sit-ting on the curb, A chirp-ing and a burp-ing And a-eat-ing dirt-y worms.

*Toidy-toid street version:*
Toidy poiple boids,
Sitt'n' on the coib,
A-choipin' and a-boipin'
And a-chewin' doity woims.

# On Mules We Find

### *(To the tune of "Auld Lang Syne")*

On mules we find
2 legs behind
and 2 we find
before.

We stand behind
before we find
what the 2 behind
be for.

When we're behind
the 2 behind,
we find what they
be for.

So stand before
the 2 behind,
behind the 2
before!

On mules we find two legs be-hind and—

two we find be-fore. We stand be-hind be-

fore we find what the two be-hind be for. When

we're be-hind the two be-hind, we find what they be

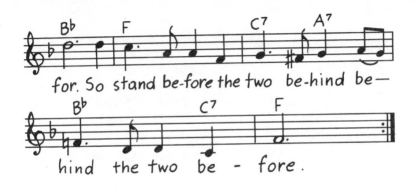

for. So stand be-fore the two be-hind be—

hind the two be - fore.

## I Don't Care for Underwear

I don't care for underwear,
I just use underroos.
I don't care for underwear,
I just use underroos.

I don't care for un-der-wear, I just use —

un-der-roos,— I don't care for un-der-wear

I just use — un - der - roos.

# Black Socks

Black socks, they never get dirty.
The longer you wear them, the stronger they get.
Sometimes I think I should launder them,
Something keeps telling me,
"Don't wash them yet—not yet—not yet!"

# 5. GREAT OLDIES

# Young Folks, Old Folks

**Chorus**  Young folks, old folks,
Everybody come.
Come to the meeting house
And have a lot of fun.

Please check your chewing gum
And raisins at the door,
And I'll tell you Bible stories
That you never heard before.

CHORUS

Young folks, old folks, Ev-r'y-bod-y come,

Come to the meet-ing house and have a lot of fun.

Please check your chew-ing gum and

rai - sins at the door, and I'll

tell you Bi-ble sto-ries that you nev-er heard be-fore.

*Sing the chorus after every 2 verses.*

Salomey was a dancer and
She danced the hoochy kooch.
She danced before the King
And he liked it very mooch.

The Queen said, "Salomey,
We'll have no scandal here,"
Soo "Whoops," said Salomey,
And she kicked the chandelier.

Sa - lo-mey was a dan-cer and she
danced the hoo-chy kooch, She danced be-fore the King and he
liked it ve-ry mooch. The Queen said "Sa-lo-mey, we'll
have no scan-dal here," Soo – "Whoops," said Sa-lo-mey and she
kicked the chan - de - lier.

57

The world was built in six days,
And finished on the seventh.
According to the contract,
It should have been the eleventh.

The masons they got tired,
And the carpenters wouldn't work,
So the only thing that they could do
Was fill it up with dirt.

Adam was the first man,
And Eve she was his spouse.
They got themselves together,
And they started keeping house.

One day they had a son—
And Abel was his name,
And everything went fine until
They started raising Cain.

Adam was a good man.
Children he had seven.
Thought he'd hire a donkey cart
And take them all to heaven.

Strange to say, he lost the way,
Although he knew it well,
And  over went the donkey cart,
And sent them all to hell.

Jonah was a sailor,
He set out for a sail.
He took a first-class passage
On a transatlantic whale.

He didn't like his quarters,
Although they were the best,
So Jonah pushed the button
And the whaley did the rest.

David was a wise guy,
A wiry little cuss.
Along came Goliath,
A-looking for a fuss.

David fetched a stone,
And conked him on the dome,
And Goliath heard the birdies singing,
"Home sweet home."

Sampson was a strong man,
You bet he was no fool.
He killed ten thousand Philistines
With the jawbone of a mule.

A woman named Delilah,
She cut his hair real thin,
And when he came to afterwards,
The coppers pulled him in.

# It Ain't Gonna Rain No More

**Chorus**

Oh, it ain't gonna rain no more,
    no more,
It ain't gonna rain no more.
So how the heck you gonna wash
    your neck,
If it ain't gonna rain no more.

CHORUS
F

Oh, it ain't gon-na rain no more, no more, It

C

ain't gon - na rain no more. So

C⁷

how the heck you gon-na wash your neck, If it

F

ain't gon - na rain no more.

*Sing the chorus after every verse.*

Oh, a peanut sat on a railroad track.
Its heart was all a-flutter.
Along came the 5:05—
Oops—peanut butter.

A cow walked on the railroad track.
The train was coming fast.
The train got off the railroad track
To let the cow go past.

Oh, there ain't no bugs on me,
There ain't no bugs on me.
There may be bugs on some of you mugs,
But there ain't no bugs on me.


A boy stood on a burning deck.
His feet were full of blisters.
He tore his pants on a rusty nail,
And now he wears his sister's.


There ain't no flies on me,
There ain't no flies on me,
There may be flies on some of you guys,
But there ain't no flies on me!


I woke up in the morning.
I glanced upon the wall.
The roaches and the bedbugs
Were having a game of ball.

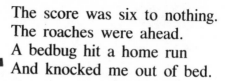

The score was six to nothing.
The roaches were ahead.
A bedbug hit a home run
And knocked me out of bed.

The monkey swings
    by the end of his tail,
And jumps from
    tree to tree.
There may be ape
    on somebody's tape,
But there ain't no ape in me.

Oh, a skinny woman took a bath.
She didn't tell a soul.
She forgot to put the stopper in,
And slid right down the hole.

Oh, a man was standing by a sewer,
And by a sewer he died.
They took him to his funeral
And called it sewer-side!

There ain't no crumbs on me,
There ain't no crumbs on me,
There may be crumbs on some of
    you bums,
But there ain't no crumbs on me!

# A Sailor Went to Sea

A sailor went to sea sea sea
To see what he could see see see,
But all that he could see see see
Was the bottom of the deep blue sea sea sea.

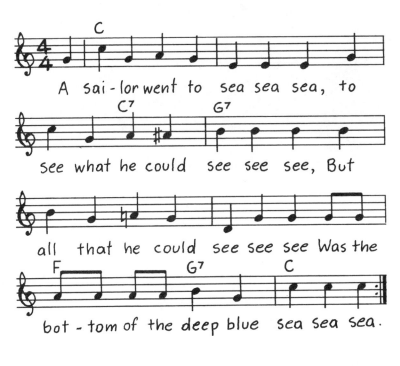

A sai-lor went to sea sea sea, to
see what he could see see see, But
all that he could see see see Was the
bot - tom of the deep blue sea sea sea.

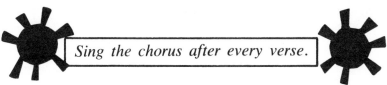

*Sing the chorus after every verse.*

Oh, Helen had a steamboat,
The steamboat had a bell,
When Helen went to heaven
The steamboat went to —

Hello, operator,
Just give me number 9.
If the line is busy
I'll kick your big —

Behind the old piano,
There was a piece of glass,
Helen slipped upon it
And hurt her little —

Ask me for a muffin,
I'll give you some old bread
And if you do not like it,
Just go and soak your head.

## What Did Delaware, Boys?

Oh, what did Delaware, boys, oh, what
    did Delaware?
Oh, what did Delaware, boys, oh, what
    did Delaware?
Oh, what did Delaware, boys, oh, what
    did Delaware?
I ask you now as a personal friend, what
    did Delaware?

Oh, what did Del - a - ware, boys, oh

what did Del-a-ware? Oh, what did Del-a-ware, boys, oh, what did Del-a-ware? Oh, what did Del-a-ware, boys, oh what did Del-a-ware? I ask you now as a per-son-al friend, what did Del-a-ware?

She wore her New Jersey, boys, she
wore her New Jersey.
She wore her New Jersey, boys, she
wore her New Jersey.
She wore her New Jersey, boys, she
wore her New Jersey.
I tell you now as a personal friend, she
wore her New Jersey.

*Sing the chorus after every verse.*

And it goes on and on with verses for at least 14
states: Try these:

*Florida:* Oh, how did FLORI-DIE *(Flora die)*, boys?
*Missouri:* She died in MISSOURI *(misery)*, boys.
*Iowa:* Oh, what does IO-WA *(Io weigh)*, boys?
*Washington:* She weighs a WASHING-TON, boys.
*Idaho:* Oh, what does IDA-HO *(Ida hoe)*, boys?
*Maryland:* She hoes her MARY-LAND, boys.
*Tennessee:* Oh, what does TENNES-SEE, boys?
*Arkansas:* She sees what ARKAN-SAS
        *(Arkan saw)*, boys.
*Oregon:* Oh, where has ORE-GON *(Ore-gone)*, boys?
*Oklahoma:* She's gone to OKLA-HOMA
        *(Okla-hom-a)*, boys.
*Massachusetts:* Oh, what did MASSA-CHEW, boys?
*Connecticut:* She chewed her
        CONNECTI-CUD, boys.

# 6. CRAZIES!

# Boom Boom

Way down south where the cotton grows,
A cockroach stepped on an elephant's toes.
The elephant said, with tears in his eyes,
"Why don't you pick on someone your own size?"

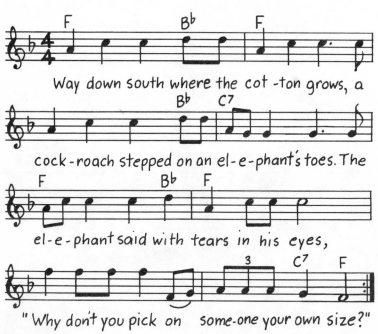

## Chorus

Boom boom, ain't it great to be cra-zy?
Boom boom, ain't it great to be nuts?
Giddy and foolish all the day long,
Boom boom, ain't it great to be cra-zy!

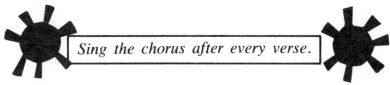

*Sing the chorus after every verse.*

I bought a suit of combination underwear,
Can't get if off, I do declare.
Wore it six months without exaggeration.
Can't get it off, 'cause I lost the combination.

69

Way up north where there's ice and snow,
There lived a penguin, name of Joe.
He got so tired of black and white,
He wore technicolor pants to the dance last night.


I love myself—I think I'm grand.
When I go to the movies I hold my hand.
I put my arm around my waist,
And when I get fresh, I slap my face.


I call myself on the telephone.
Just to hear my musical tone.
I ask myself for a heavy date.
And I pick myself up at half-past eight.


Up in the north and a long way off,
A donkey got the whooping cough.
He coughed so hard, his head fell off—
Up in the north and a long way off.

Fuzzy Wuzzy was a bear,
And Fuzzy Wuzzy
    cut his hair,
So Fuzzy Wuzzy
    wasn't fuzzy.
No, by Jove, he wasn't,
    wuz he?

I take a swim in my swimming pool.
I jump from the board, 'cause that's the rule.
I hit my head on cement and mortar.
Forgot to look—there was no water!


That one-eared cat, who used to sit
Watching grandma rock and knit,
Swallowed a ball of bright red yarn—
And out came her kittens with red sweaters on.


A horse and a flea and three blind mice
Sat on a tombstone, eating rice.
The horse he slipped and fell on the flea.
"Whoops," said the flea, "there's a horse on me!"

# A Horse Named Bill

I had a horse, his name was Bill,
And when he ran, he couldn't stand still.
He ran away one day,
And also I ran with him.

He ran so hard, he couldn't stop,
He ran into a barber shop.
He fell exhausted with his teeth
In the barber's left shoulder.

Oh, I went out into the woods last year,
To hunt for fleas and not for deer,
Because I am—no, I ain't—
The world's best sharpshooter.

At shooting ducks I am a beaut.
There is no duck I cannot shoot,
In the eye, in the ear,
In the index finger.

In Frisco Bay there lives a whale
And she eats pork chops by the pail,
By the hatbox, by the pillbox,
By the hogshead and schooner.

Her name is Lena, she's a peach,
But don't leave food within her reach,
Or babies, or nursemaids,
Or chocolate ice cream sodas.

She loves to laugh, and when she smiles,
You just see teeth for miles and miles,
And tonsils, and spareribs
And things too fierce to mention.

She knows no games so when she plays,
She rolls her eyes for days and days,
She vibrates and yodels
And breaks the Ten Commandments.

Oh, what can you do in a case like that?
Oh, what can you do but stamp on your hat?
Or on an eggshell or a toothbrush
Or anything that's helpless!

# Do Your Ears Hang Low?

Do your ears hang low?
Do they wobble to and fro?
Can you tie them in a knot?
Can you tie them in a bow?
Can you toss them over your
       shoulder
Like a continental soldier?
Do your ears—hang—low?

Do your ears hang low? Do they
wob-ble to and fro? Can you tie them in a
knot? Can you tie them in a bow? Can you
toss them o-ver your shoul-der like a
con-tin-ent-al sol-dier, Do your ears hang low?—

Yes, my ears hang low.
They can wobble to and fro,
I can tie them in a knot,
I can tie them in a bow,
I can toss them over my shoulder
Like a continental soldier.
Yes, my ears—hang—low.

# Three Ways to Get Peanut Butter Off the Roof of Your Mouth

*(Say this very solemnly.)*
There are 3 ways to get peanut butter off the roof of
your mouth. One way is to shake your head back and
forth.
    *(Shake your head vigorously.)*
If that doesn't work, you could kind of whistle.
    *(Whistle.)*
If that doesn't work, you could scrape it off with your
first finger.
    *(Scrape it off.)*
There are 3 ways to get peanut butter off your finger.
One way is to shake it off.
    *(Shake finger vigorously.)*
Another way is to blow it off.
    *(Try blowing it off.)*
If that doesn't work, you can scrape it off with your 2
front teeth.
    *(Scrape it off with your 2 front teeth.)*
There are 3 ways to get peanut butter off the roof of
your mouth *(and on and on and on)*.

# I Am Slowly Going Crazy

I am slowly going crazy,
I am slowly going crazy,
I am slowly going crazy,
But they haven't got me
    locked up yet!

(*spoken*) NOT YET!

I am slow-ly go-ing cra - zy,

I am slow-ly go-ing cra - zy,

I am slow-ly go-ing cra-zy but they

have-n't got me locked up yet *(spoken)* NOT YET!

# I'm a Nut

I'm a little acorn, small and round,
Lying on the cold, cold ground.
People come and step on me.
That's why I'm so cracked, you see.

**Chorus**
I'm a nut! Tch, tch,
I'm a nut! Tch, tch,
I'm a nut! Tch, tch,
I'm a nut! Tch, tch.

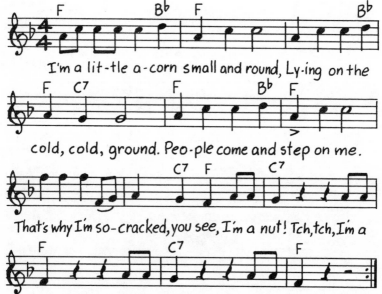

# Michael Finnegan

I know a man named Michael Finnegan.
He had whiskers on his chin-igin.
The wind blew them off, but they grew in
    again,
Poor old Michael Finnegan (begin again)—

I know a man named
Mi-chael Fin-ne-gan. He had whis-kers
on his chin-i-gin. The wind blew them off but
they grew in a-gain, Poor old Mi-chael
Fin-ne-gan (be-gin a-gain)

I know a man named Michael Finnegan.
He went fishing with a pin-agin,
Caught a fish and dropped it in-agin,
Poor old Michael Finnegan (begin again)—

I know a man named Michael Finnegan.
Climbed a tree and barked his shin-agin,
Took off several yards of skin-igin,
Poor old Michael Finnegan (begin again)—

I know a man named Michael Finnegan.
He kicked up an awful din-igin,
Because they said he could not sing-igin,
Poor old Michael Finnegan (begin again)—

I know a man named Michael Finnegan.
He got fat and then got thin again,
Then he died and had to begin again,
Poor old Michael Finnegan (begin again)—

# 7. SO YOU THOUGHT YOU KNEW ALL THE WORDS!

# Miss Lucy

Miss Lucy had a baby.
She named him Tiny Tim.
She put him in the bathtub
To see if he could swim.

Miss Lu - cy had a ba-by, She named him Ti - ny Tim. She put him in the bath - tub, To see if he could swim.

He drank up all the water,
He ate up all the soap,
He tried to eat the bathtub
But it wouldn't go down his throat.

He floated up the river.
He floated down the lake.
And now Miss Lucy's baby
Has got a bellyache.

Miss Lucy called the Doctor,
Miss Lucy called the Nurse,
Miss Lucy called the lady
With the alligator purse.

"Measles," said the Doctor,
"Mumps," said the Nurse,
"A virus," said the lady
With the alligator purse.

"Penicillin," said the Doctor,
"Bed rest," said the Nurse,
"Pizza," said the lady
With the alligator purse.

"He'll live," said the Doctor,
"He's all right," said the Nurse,
"I'm leaving," said the lady
With the alligator purse.

Miss Lucy gave me peaches,
And then she gave me pears,
And then she gave me fifty cents
And kicked me up the stairs.

My mother was born in England,
My father was born in France,
And I was born in diapers
Because I had no pants.

# Turkey in the Straw

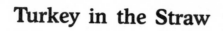

**Chorus**
Turkey in the straw
    (turkey in the straw),
Turkey in the hay
    (turkey in the hay),
Roll 'em up and twist 'em
    with a high tuck-a-haw,
And hit 'em with a tune
    they call "Turkey in the Straw!"

I went out— to— milk— and I

did-n't know-how so I milked the goat- in—

stead of the cow. Saw a tur— key—sit-tin' on a

pile—of— straw, A— wink-in'— at— his—

I went out to milk and I didn't know how,
So I milked the goat instead of the cow.
Saw a turkey sittin' on a pile of straw,
A-winkin' at his mother-in-law.

moth-er-in-law. Tur-key in the straw
(Tur-key in the straw), Tur-key in the hay
(Tur-key in the hay), Roll 'em up and twist 'em with a
high tuck-a-haw, And hit 'em with a tune-they call
Tur-key in the straw!

*Sing the chorus after every verse.*

I met an old catfish, swimmin' in the stream.
I asked that old catfish, "What do you mean?"
I grabbed that catfish right by the snout,
And turned Mister Catfish wrong side out!

Oh, I went to Toledo and I walked around the block,
And I walked right into the baker's shop.
And I took two doughnuts out of the grease,
And I handed the lady there a five-cent piece.


Oh, she looked at the nickel, and she looked at me,
And she said, "This money is no good, you see.
There's a hole in the middle and it goes right
        through."
Says I, "There's a hole in the doughnut, too!"


Well, if frogs had wings and snakes had hair
And cars went a-flying through the air—
Well, if watermelons grew on the huckleberry vine,
We'd all have winter in the summertime.


I love to go a-fishin' on a bright summer day,
To see the perches and the catfish play,
With their hands in their pockets and their
        pockets in their pants.
Oh, I love to see the fishes do the
        hootchie-kootchie dance!

# Clementine

In a cavern, in a canyon,
Excavating for a mine,
Lived a miner forty-niner
And his daughter, Clementine.

**Chorus**
Oh, my darling, oh, my darling,
Oh, my darling Clementine,
You are lost and gone forever,
Dreadful sorry, Clementine.

In a ca-vern, in a can-yon, ex-ca-va-ting for a
mine, Lived a min-er, for-ty nin-er, And his
daugh-ter, Cle-men-tine, Oh my dar-ling, Oh my
dar-ling, Oh my dar-ling Cle-men-tine, You are
lost and gone for-e-ver, Dread-ful sor-ry, Cle-men-tine.

*Sing the chorus after every verse.*

Light she was and like a fairy,
And her shoes were number nine,
Herring boxes without topses,
Sandals were for Clementine.

Drove her ducklings to the water,
Every morning just at nine,
Hit her foot against a splinter,
Fell into the foaming brine.

Ruby lips above the water,
Blowing bubbles soft and fine,
But alas, I was no swimmer
So I lost my Clementine.

Then the miner, forty-niner,
Soon began to peak and pine,
Thought he oughta join his daughter,
Now he's with his Clementine.

There's a churchyard on the hillside,
Where the flowers grow and twine,
There grow roses, 'mongst the posies,
Fertilized by Clementine.

In my dreams she still doth haunt me,
Robed in garlands soaked in brine,
Though in life I used to hug her,
Now she's dead, I draw the line.

Now you scouts may learn the moral
Of this little tale of mine,
Artificial respiration
Would have saved my Clementine.

How I missed her, how I missed her,
How I missed my Clementine,
Till I kissed her little sister,
And forgot my Clementine.

# You Can't Get to Heaven

Oh, you can't get to heaven
    (oh, you can't get to heaven)
On roller skates
    (on roller skates)
You'll roll right by
    (you'll roll right by)
Those pearly gates
    (those pearly gates)

ain't a-gon-na grieve— my Lord no more.——

### Chorus
Oh, you can't get to heaven
On roller skates—
You'll roll right by
Those pearly gates—
I ain't a-gonna grieve
My Lord no more.
I ain't a-gonna grieve my Lord no more,
I ain't a-gonna grieve my Lord no more,
I ain't a-gonna grieve my Lord no more.

CHORUS

I ain't a-gon-na grieve my Lord no more, I
ain't a-gon-na grieve my Lord no more, I
ain't a-gon-na grieve—— my Lord
no more.——

*Sing the chorus after each verse, substituting each new thing that you "can't get to heaven" in.*

Oh, you can't get to heaven
In a rocking chair.
'Cause the rocking chair
Won't take you there.

Oh, you can't get to heaven
In a trolley car,
'Cause the gosh darn thing
Won't go that far.

Oh, you can't get to heaven
On a rocket ship,
'Cause a rocket ship
Won't make the trip.

Oh, you can't get to heaven
With powder and paint,
'Cause the Lord don't want
You as you ain't.

Oh, you can't get to heaven,
In a limousine,
'Cause the Lord don't sell
No gasoline.

You can't chew tobaccy
On that golden shore,
'Cause the Lord don't have
No cuspidor.

Oh, you can't get to heaven
With Superman,
'Cause the Lord he is
A Batman fan.

Oh, the devil is mad
And I am glad,
He lost a soul,
He thought he had.

Oh, you can't get to heaven,
On a pair of skis,
'Cause you'll schuss right through
St. Peter's knees.

Oh, you can't get to heaven
With a pizza pie
'Cause the pizza pie
Won't go that high.

If you get to heaven
Before I do,
Just bore a hole
And pull me through.

If I get to heaven
Before you do,
I'll plug that hole
With shavings and glue!

"That's all there is—
There ain't no more,"
St. Peter said,
And closed the door.

# 8. TO THE TUNE OF...

# Bring Back My Neighbors to Me

*(To the tune of "My Bonnie Lies Over the Ocean")*

One night as I lay on my pillow,
One night as I lay on my bed,
I stuck my feet out of the window,
Next morning my neighbors were dead.

One night as I lay on my pil-low,— One night as I lay on my bed,—— I stuck my feet out of the win-dow, — Next morn-ing my neigh-bors were dead. Bring back, bring back, Oh bring back my neigh-bors to me, to me.

96

Bring back, bring back, Oh bring back my neigh-bors to me.

### Chorus

Bring back, bring back,
Oh, bring back my neighbors to me, to me.
Bring back, bring back,
Oh, bring back my neighbors to me.

 *Sing the chorus after every verse.*

One day as I sat in my rocker,
One day as I sat very still,
A firecracker killed off my neighbors,
And made me exceedingly ill.

My neighbors looked into the gas tank,
But nothing inside could they see.
They lighted a match to assist them,
Oh, bring back my neighbors to me!

# The Wrong End
### (To the tune of "My Bonnie Lies Over the Ocean")

Oh, rabbits have bright, shiny noses,
I'm telling you this as a friend.
The reason their noses are shiny:
The powder puff's on the wrong end.

Wrong end—wrong end—
The powder puff's
     on the wrong end—
Wrong end—

Wrong end—wrong end—
The powder puff's
     on the wrong end!

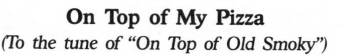

# On Top of My Pizza
### (To the tune of "On Top of Old Smoky")

On top of my pizza—
All covered with sauce—
Could not find the mushrooms,
I think they got lost.

I looked in the closet,
I looked in the sink,
I looked in the cup that
Held my cola drink.

I looked in the saucepan,
Right under the lid,
No matter where I looked,
Those mushrooms stayed hid.

Next time you make pizza,
I'm begging you, please,
Do not give me mushrooms,
But just plain old cheese.

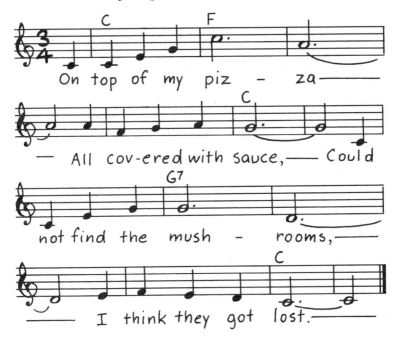

On top of my piz - za —
— All cov-ered with sauce, — Could
not find the mush - rooms, —
— I think they got lost. —

# I Went Into the Water

*(To the tune of "Battle Hymn of the Republic")*

Oh, I went into the water,
And I got my feet all wet.
I went into the water,
And I got my feet all wet.
I went into the water,
And I got my feet all wet.
But I didn't get my *(clap, clap)* wet—yet.

Oh, I went into the water,
And I got my ankles wet.
I went into the water,
And I got my ankles wet.
I went into the water,
And I got my ankles wet.
But I didn't get my *(clap, clap)* wet—yet.

Oh, I went into the water,
And I got my legs all wet.
    *(and so on, up to your head)*

**Last stanza:**
Oh, I went into the water,
But I didn't get it wet.
I went into the water,
But I didn't get it wet.
I went into the water,
But I didn't get it wet.
I didn't get my camera wet.

# Christopher McCracken

*(To the tune of "Battle Hymn of the Republic")*

Christopher McCracken went a-fishing
    for some crabs,
Christopher McCracken went a-fishing
    for some crabs,
Christopher McCracken went a-fishing
    for some crabs,
But he didn't catch a (*clap, clap*) crab.

Oh, all he caught was some old virus,
All he caught was some old virus,
All he caught was some old virus,
But he didn't catch a (*clap, clap*) crab.

# I Was Only Fooling
### (To the tune of "Battle Hymn of the Republic")

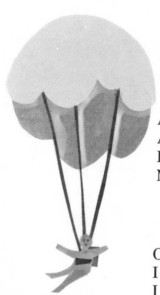

I wear my silk pajamas
In the summer when it's hot,
And I wear my flannel nightie
In the winter when it's not.

And sometimes in the springtime
And sometimes in the fall,
I slip between the covers with
Nothing on at all.

**Chorus**
Oh, I was only only foolin',
I was only only foolin',
I was only only foolin'
About the springtime and the fall.

I blast off in my rocket ship to visit on the moon,
And when I drive my submarine, I sing a silly tune,
And when I use my parachute, I float so gently down
And land with a bump in my own home town.

**Chorus**
I was only foolin',
I was only foolin',
I was only foolin'
About my own home town.

*More verses:*

It was midnight on the ocean,
Not a taxi in sight.
The sun was shining brightly,
And it rained all day that night.

Please don't ask me any questions,
I will make no more suggestions.
Please don't ask me any questions,
And I'll tell you no more lies.

## The Flea Fly Song
*(To the tune of "Battle Hymn of the Republic")*

One flea fly flew up the flu and
  the other flea fly flew down.
Oh, one flea fly flew up the flu
  and the other flea fly flew down.
Oh, one flea fly flew up the flu and
  the other flea fly flew down.
Oh, one flea fly flew up the flu
  and the other flea fly flew down.

**Chorus**

They were only playing flu fly,
They were only playing flu fly,
They were only playing flu fly
In the springtime and the fall.

# The Grasshopper Song

*(To the tune of "Battle Hymn of the Republic")*

The first grasshopper jumped right
over the second grasshopper's back.
Oh, the first grasshopper jumped right
over the second grasshopper's back.
The first grasshopper jumped right over
the second grasshopper's back.
Oh, the first grasshopper jumped right
over the second grasshopper's back.

**Chorus**

They were only playing leap frog,
They were only playing leap frog,
They were only playing leap frog,
In the springtime and the fall.

# I Had a Silly Chicken
### (To the tune of "Turkey in the Straw")

Oh, I had a silly chicken
And he wouldn't lay an egg,
So I poured hot water
Up and down his leg,
And he sang a silly song
Which turned out to be a ballad,
And my chicken laid a sandwich
Filled with egg and tuna (tune o') salad.

Oh, I had a silly chicken
He went scratching in the dirt,
And he scratched so hard
That his feet—they hurt.
So he bandaged them way up
From the thigh bone to his toe.
And you should have seen that chicken
Do a do-si-do!

Oh, I had a silly chicken
And he wouldn't lay an egg,
So I poured hot water
Up and down his leg,
And he giggled and he giggled,
And he giggled all the day,
And my poor little chicken
Laid a hard-boiled egg!

## The Horse Went Around
*(To the tune of "Turkey in the Straw")*

Oh, the horse went around
With his foot off the ground.
Oh, the horse went around
With his foot off the ground.
Oh, the horse went around
With his foot off the ground.
Oh, the horse went around
With his foot off the ground.

## Chorus

*(spoken)* Next verse
Same as the first.
A little bit louder
And a little bit worse.

*Sing the chorus after every verse.*

Oh, the horse went around
With his foot off _____ .
Oh, the horse went around
With his foot off _____ .
Oh, the horse went around
With his foot off _____ .
Oh, the horse went around
With his foot off _____ .

Oh, the horse went around
With his foot off the _____ .
Oh, the horse went around
With his foot off the _____ .
Oh, the horse went around
With his foot off the _____ .
Oh, the horse went around
With his foot off the _____ .

Sing the song 9 times, leaving out the last word each time, until, finally, you're singing in total silence. After this, sing the entire song aloud once again.

# Found a Peanut

*(To the tune of "Clementine")*

Found a peanut, found a peanut,
Found a peanut last night.
Last night I found a peanut,
Found a peanut last night.

Broke it open, broke it open,
Broke it open last night.
Last night I broke it open,
Broke it open last night.

Found it rotten, found it rotten,
Found it rotten last night.
Last night I found it rotten
Found it rotten last night.

Ate it anyway, ate it anyway,
Ate it anyway last night.
Last night I ate it anyway,
Ate it anyway, last night.

Got a tummyache, got a tummyache,
Got a tummyache last night.
Last night I got a tummyache,
Got a tummyache last night.

Called the doctor, called the doctor,
Called the doctor last night.
Last night I called the doctor,
Called the doctor last night.

An operation, an operation,
An operation last night.
Last night an operation,
An operation last night.

Died anyway, died anyway,
Died anyway last night.
Last night I died anyway,
Died anyway last night.

Went to heaven, went to heaven,
Went to heaven last night.
Last night I went to heaven,
Went to heaven last night.

Wouldn't take me, wouldn't take me,
Wouldn't take me last night.
Last night they wouldn't take me,
Wouldn't take me last night.

Went the other way, went the other way,
Went the other way last night.
Last night I went the other way,
Went the other way last night.

Found it all a dream, found it all a dream,
Found it all a dream last night.
Last night I found it all a dream,
Found it all a dream last night.

Found a peanut, found a peanut,
Found a peanut last night.
Last night I found a peanut,
Found a peanut last night.

# Birds in the Wilderness

*(To the tune of "The Old Grey Mare")*

Here we sit like birds in the wilderness,
Birds in the wilderness,
Birds in the wilderness,
Here we sit like birds in the wilderness,
Waiting for our food.

# 9. FUN TO SING

# Baby Bumble Bee

Oh, I'm bringing home a baby bumble
bee,
Won't my mommy be so proud of me,
'Cause I'm bringing home a baby
bumble bee—
Buzzy, buzzy, buzzy—
*(spoken)* OOOOH, it bit me!

Oh, I'm bring-ing home a bab-y bum-ble bee,

Won't my mom-my be so proud of me, 'Cause I'm

bring-ing home a bab-y bum-ble bee ——

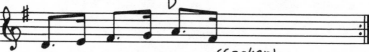

Buz-zy, buz-zy, buz-zy— *(spoken)* OOH, it bit me!

Oh, I'm bringing home a baby turtle,
Won't my mommy really pop her girdle,
'Cause I'm bringing home a baby
turtle—
Snappy, snappy, snappy—
*(spoken)* OOOOH, it bit me!

Oh, I'm bringing home a baby
    rattlesnake,
Won't my mommy shi-ver
    and shake,
'Cause I'm bringing home
    a baby rattlesnake—
Rattle, rattle, rattle—
*(spoken)* OOOOH, it bit me!

Oh, I'm bringing home a baby dinosaur,
Won't my mommy fall right through the floor,
'Cause I'm bringing home a baby dinosaur—
Gobble, gobble, gobble—
*(spoken)* OOOOH, it ate me!

# The Cat Came Back

Old Mister Johnson had troubles of his own.
He had a yellow cat and it wouldn't leave home.
He tried and he tried to give the cat away.
He gave it to a man going off to Bombay.

**Chorus**
But the cat came back the very next day.
The cat came back, thought it was a goner,
But the cat came back
'Cause it couldn't stay away.

Old Mis-ter John-son had trou-bles of his own, He

had a yel-low cat and it would-n't leave home. He

tried and he tried to give the cat a-way. He gave it to a

man— go-ing off to Bom-bay. But the cat came back, the

ve-ry next day. The cat came back, thought it was a

go-ner, but the cat came back 'cause it couldn't stay a-way.

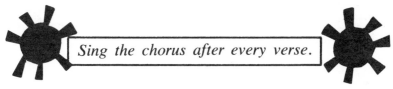

*Sing the chorus after every verse.*

He gave it to a man going way out west;
Told him to take it to the one he loved the best.
The train hit the curve, and then it jumped the rail.
Not a soul was left behind to tell the gruesome tale.


Gave it to a gambler with a dollar note.
Told him to take it up the river in a boat.
Tied a rope around its neck that must have weighed a
      pound.
Now they drag the river for the gambler that is
      drowned.

Gave it to a feller up in a balloon.
Telling him to take it to the man in the moon.
The balloon it busted and everybody said
Ten miles away they picked up that feller good and
      dead.


The farmer swore he'd kill the yellow cat on sight,
Loaded up his shotgun with nails and dynamite.
Waited and he waited for it to come around.
Ninety-seven pieces of the man is all they found.


Way across the ocean they sent the cat at last,
Vessel only out a day and taking water fast.
People all began to pray, the boat began to toss.
Great big gust of wind came by and every soul was
      lost.


On a telegraph wire, sparrows in a bunch.
Cat was feeling hungry, thought they'd be good for
      lunch.
Climbed softly up the pole, and when it reached the
      top,
Stepped on the 'lectric wire which tied it in a knot.


The cat got discouraged and thought the thing to do
Was to take a vacation upon the ocean blue.
So it took a voyage to six foreign cities,
And came home one month later with six little kitties.


Cat was a possessor of a family of its own,
With six little kittens, till there came a cyclone.
Blew the house apart and tossed the cat around.
The air was full of kittens; not one was ever found.

116

# Old Hogan's Goat

There was a man
        (there was a man),
Now please take note
        (now please take note),
There was a man
        (there was a man)
Who had a goat
        (who had a goat).
He loved that goat
        (he loved that goat),
Indeed he did
        (indeed he did).
He loved that goat
        (he loved that goat),
Just like a kid
        (just like a kid)!

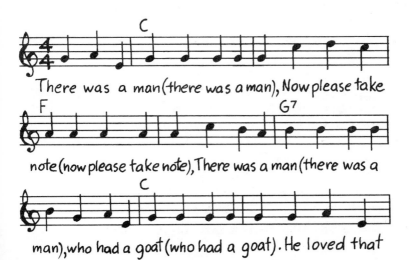

goat (he loved that goat), In-deed he

F                                   G7

did (in-deed he did). He loved that goat (he loved that

C

goat), just like a kid (just like a kid)!

One day that goat
     (one day that goat)
Was feeling fine—
     (was feeling fine—)
Ate three red shirts
     (ate three red shirts)
Right off the line.
     (right off the line).
His master came
     (his master came)
And beat his back
     (and beat his back)
And tied him to
     (and tied him to)
A railroad track.
     (a railroad track).

The whistle blew
        (too, too, too, too).
The train drew nigh.
        (the train drew nigh)
The poor goat knew
        (the poor goat knew)
That he must die.
        (that he must die).
He gave three shrieks
        (eek, eek, eek, eek)
Of mortal pain,
        (of mortal pain)
Coughed up the shirts
        (coughed up the shirts)
And flagged the train!
        (and flagged the train).

# Itchy Flea

(*spoken:*) Flea flea—
        Flea fly—Flea fly—
        Flea fly mosquito, flea fly
        mosquito!

Oh, no no no more mosquitoes,
Oh, no no no more mosquitoes,
Itchy itchy, scratchy scratchy,
Oh, I got one down my backy—
Itchy itchy, scratchy scratchy,
Oh, I got one down my backy!
Beat that big bad bug with the bug
        spray—
Beat that big bad bug with the bug
        spray—
(*spoken:*) Shhh!

Oh, no no no more mos-qui-toes, Oh, no no
no more mos-qui-toes, It-chy, it-chy, scrat-chy, scrat-chy
Oh, I got one down my back-y, It-chy, it-chy, scrat-chy, scrat-chy

120

Oh, I got one down my back-y! Beat that big bad
bug with the bug spray Beat that big bad
bug with the bug spray    Shhhh!

## Popeye the Sailor Man

I'm Popeye, the sailor man.
I live in a moving van.
I go where I'm sent
And I save on the rent,
I'm Popeye, the sailor man.

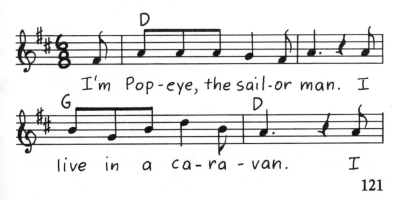

I'm Pop-eye, the sail-or man. I
live in a ca-ra-van.    I

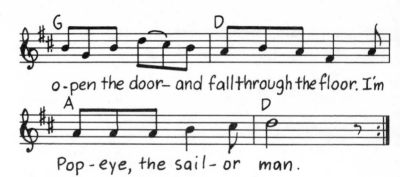

o-pen the door— and fall through the floor. I'm

Pop-eye, the sail-or man.

I'm Popeye, the sailor man.
I live in a caravan.
I open the door
And fall through the floor
I'm Popeye, the sailor man.

I'm Popeye, the sailor man.
I live in a garbage can.
It's cramped and it's crude,
But I get lots of food,
I'm Popeye, the sailor man.

I'm Popeye, the sailor man.
I'm doing the best I can.
I eat all my spinach,
I fight to the finish,
I'm Popeye, the sailor man.

# Now You May Think

Now you may think (now you may think)
That there ain't no more (that there ain't no more),
Now you may think (now you may think)
That there ain't no more (that there ain't no more),
Now you may think that there ain't no more,
Well, there ain't!

*(Well, yes, there is . . .)*

# Be Kind to Your Web-Footed Friends

Be kind to your web-footed friends,
For a duck may be somebody's mother.
They live in the bottom of the swamp,
Where the weather is cold and damp (d-ah-mp).
You may think that this is the end—
Well, it is!

Be kind to your web-foot-ed friends, for a
duck may be some-bod-y's moth - er. They
live in the bot -tom of the swamp, where the
wea-ther is cold and damp. You
may think that this is the end- Well, it is!

*(That's all, duck . . .)*

# INDEX OF FIRST LINES

**125**

# INDEX

# Guitar Chords

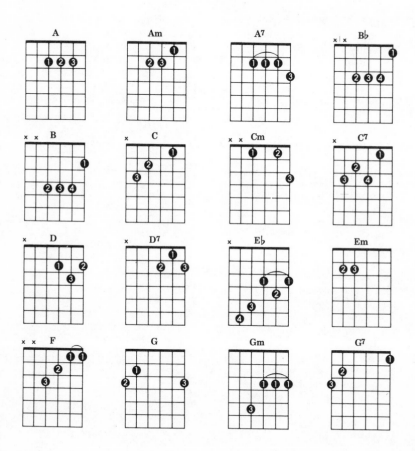